Copyright © 2025 Jennifer Jones
All copyright laws and rights reserved.
Published in the U.S.A.
For more information, email info@ninjalifehacks.tv
Paperback ISBN: 978-1-63731-930-7
Hardcover ISBN: 978-1-63731-932-1
eBook ISBN: 978-1-63731-931-4

Find the Pencil Hospital lesson plans at ninjalifehacks.tv

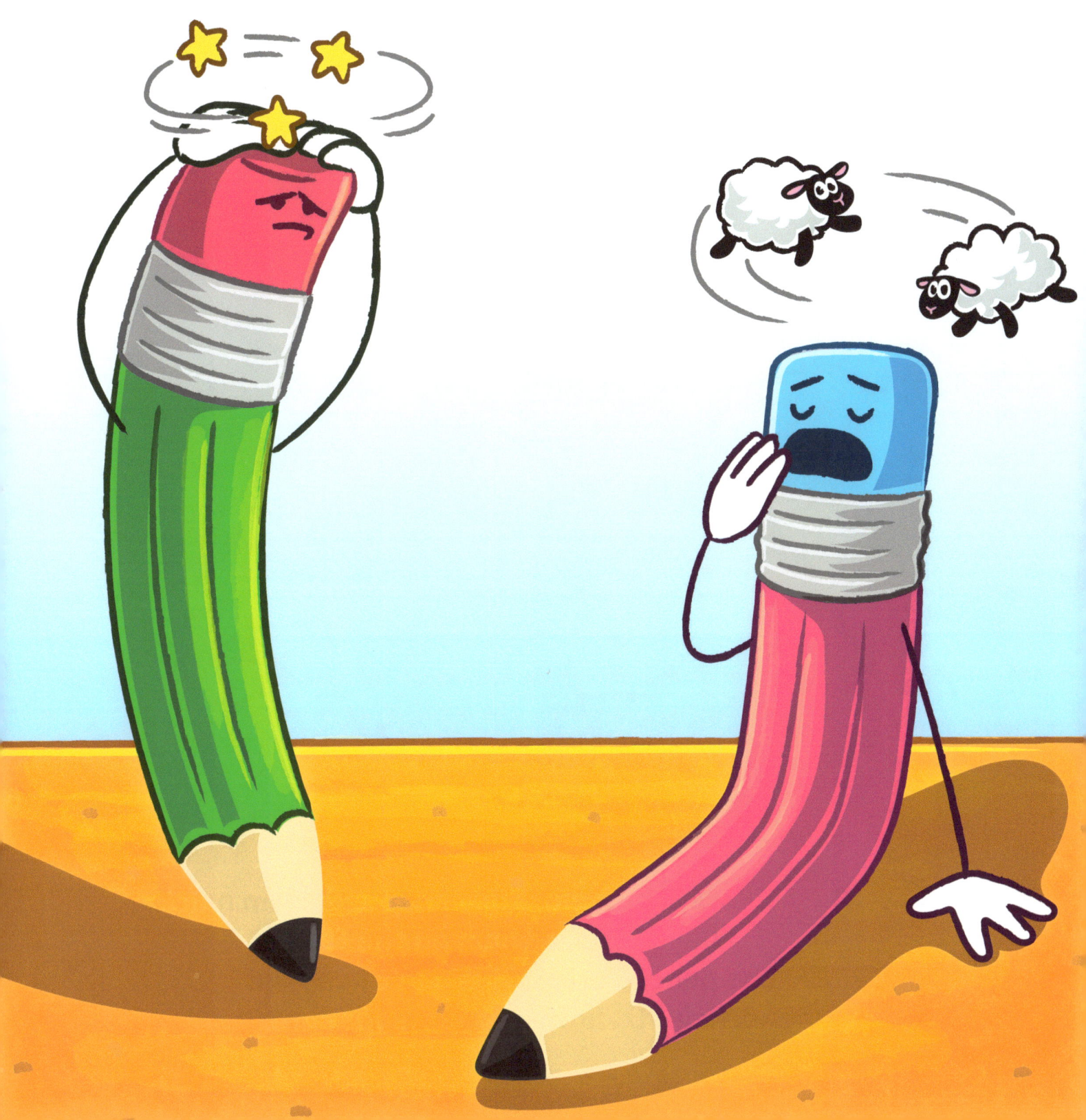

They chewed on them. They snapped them quick.
They dropped them on the floor.
The pencils cried, "We can't keep up!"
Their strength was gone for sure.

Off they went to Pencil Hospital,
where older pencils were the nurses.
They checked each pencil top to tip
and bandaged up their curses.

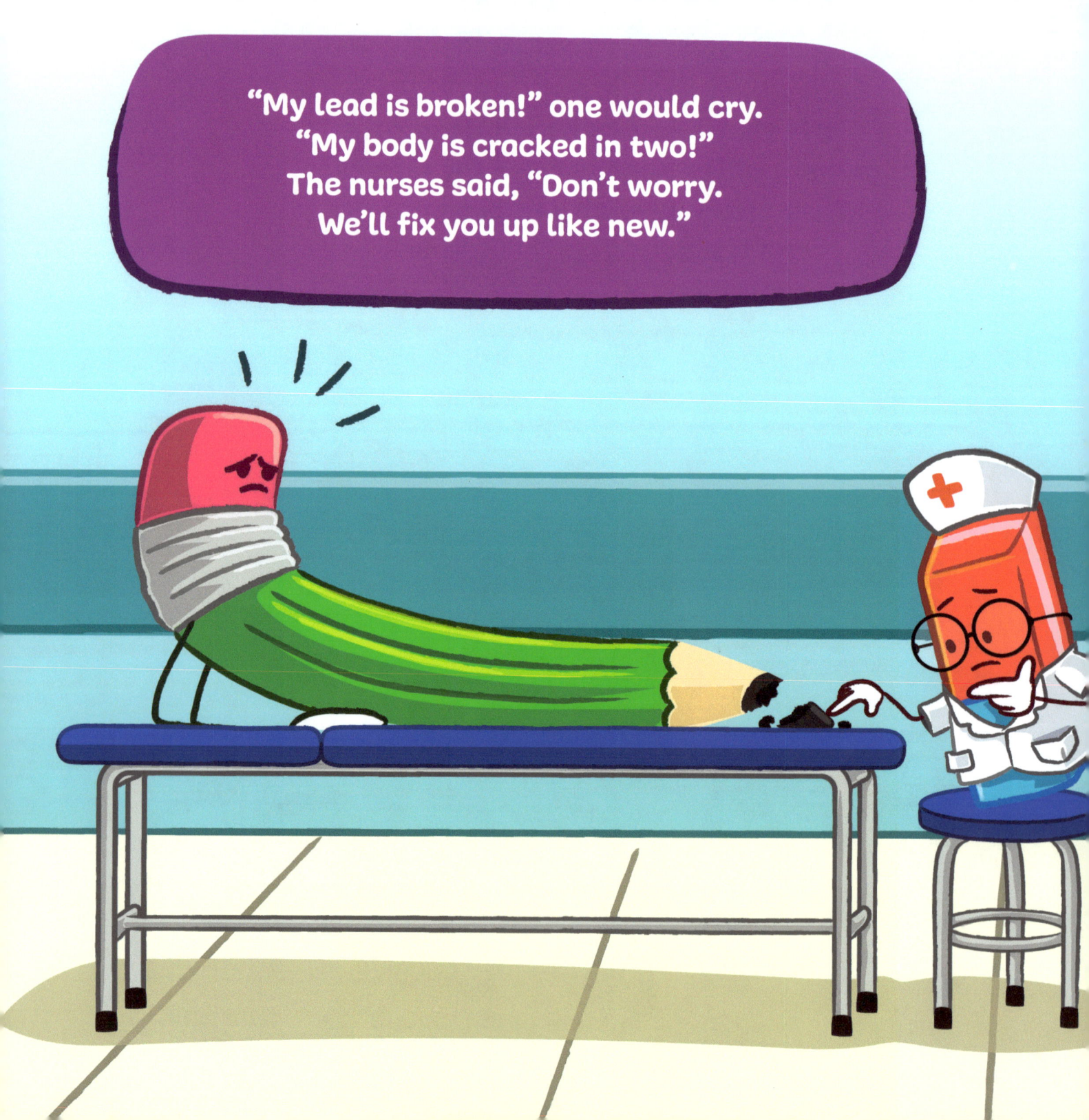

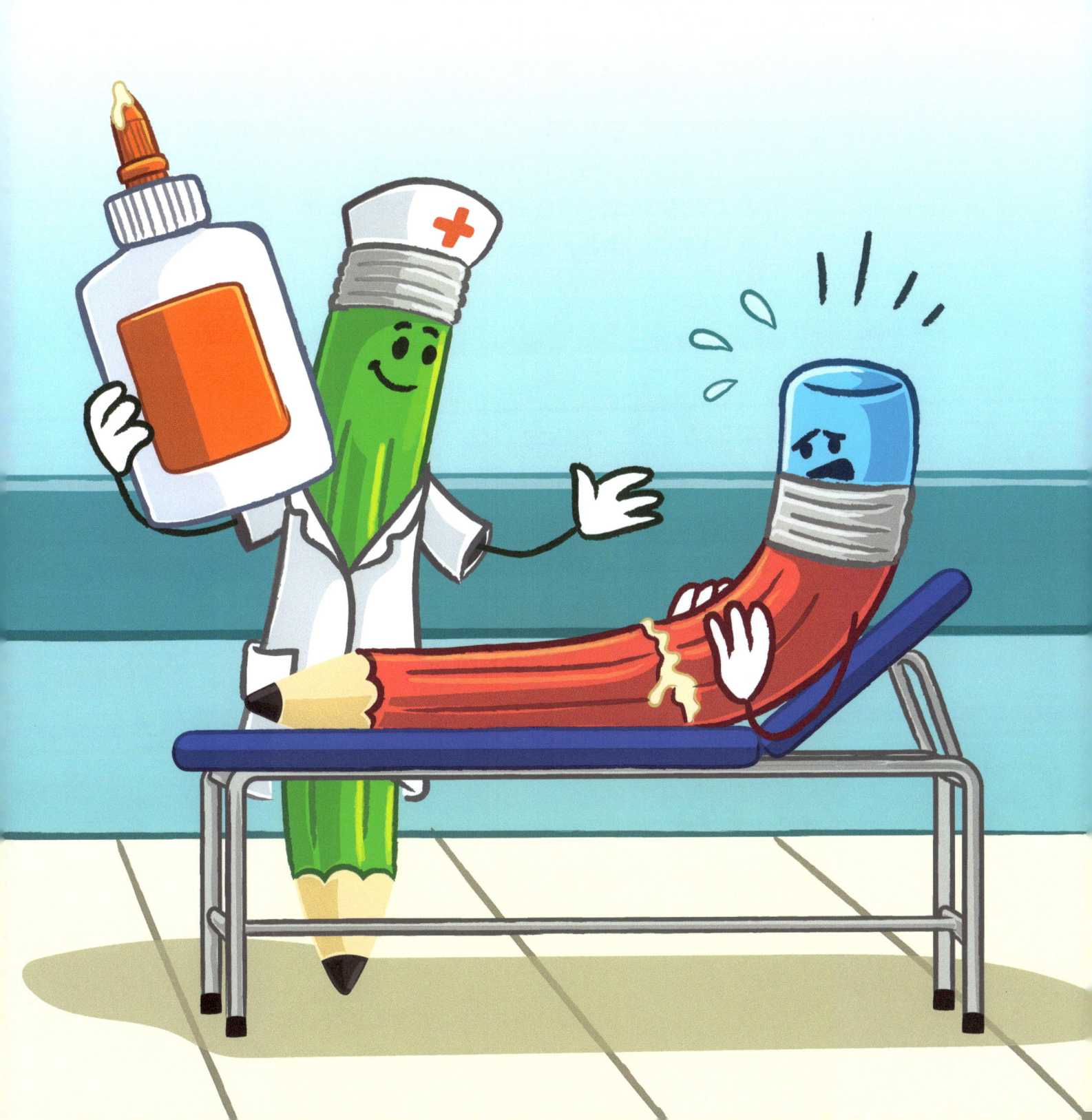

They sharpened, glued, and wrapped with care.
Each pencil got a treat.
A cozy bed and some extra rest
until they felt complete.

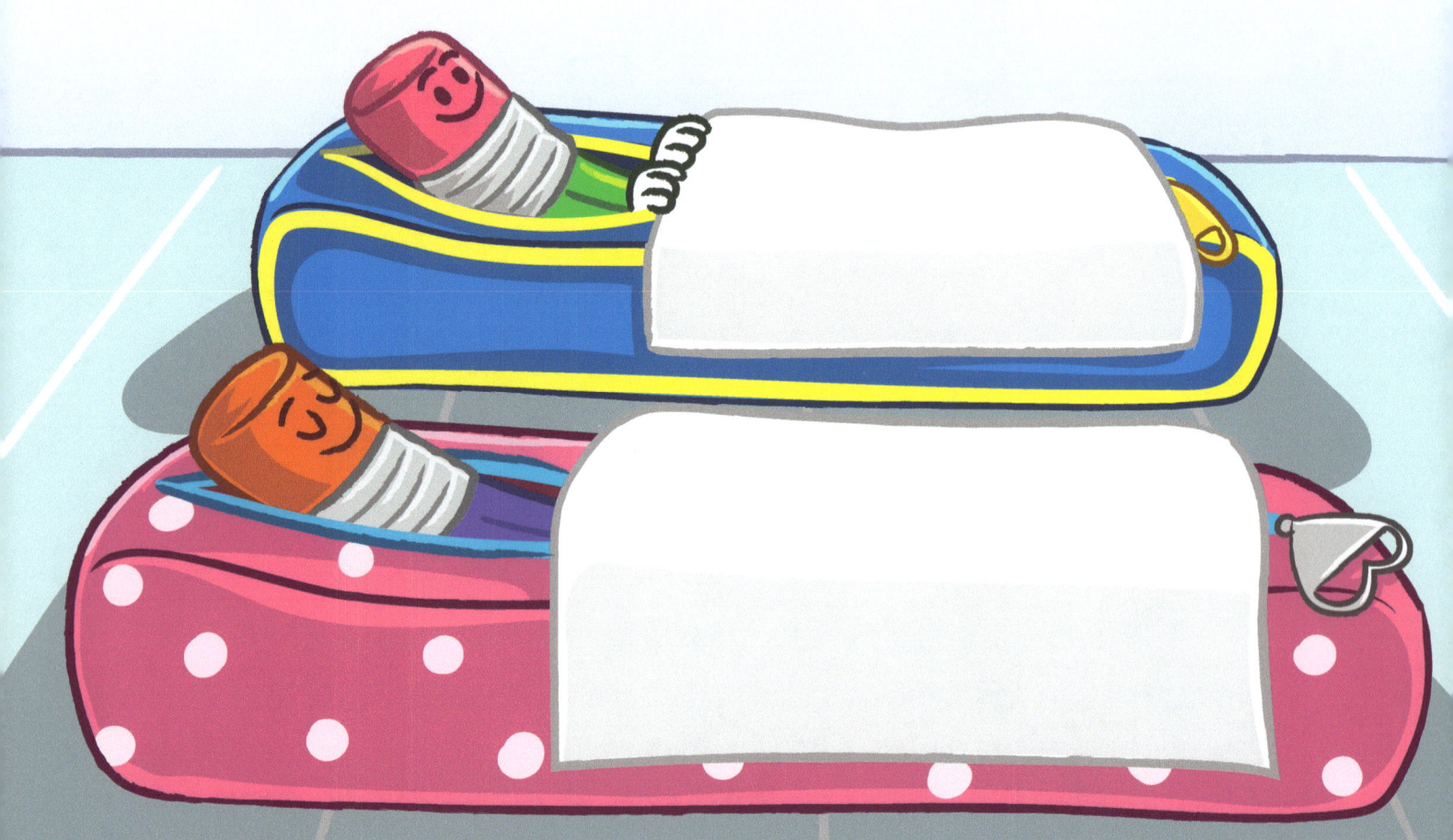

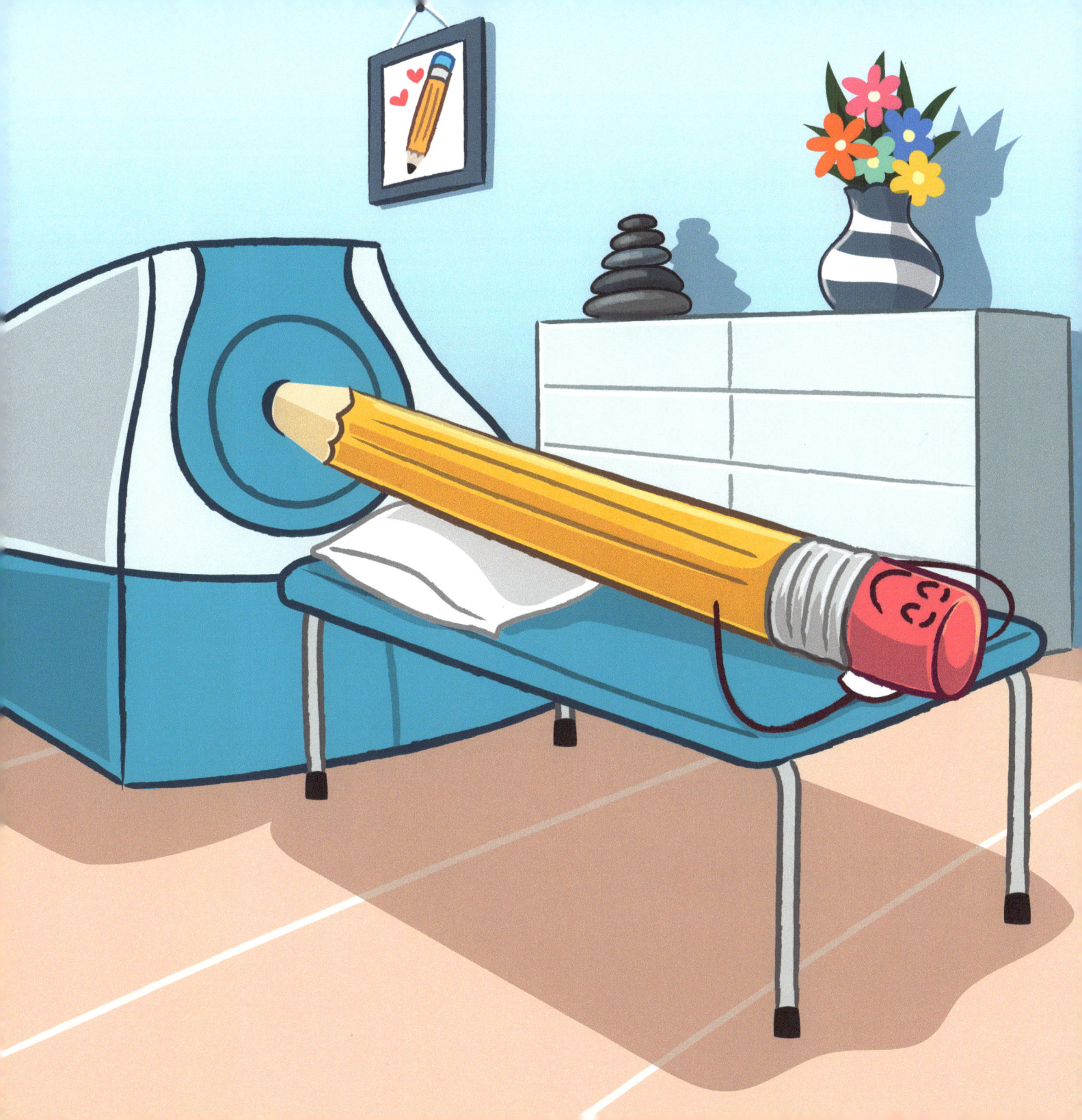

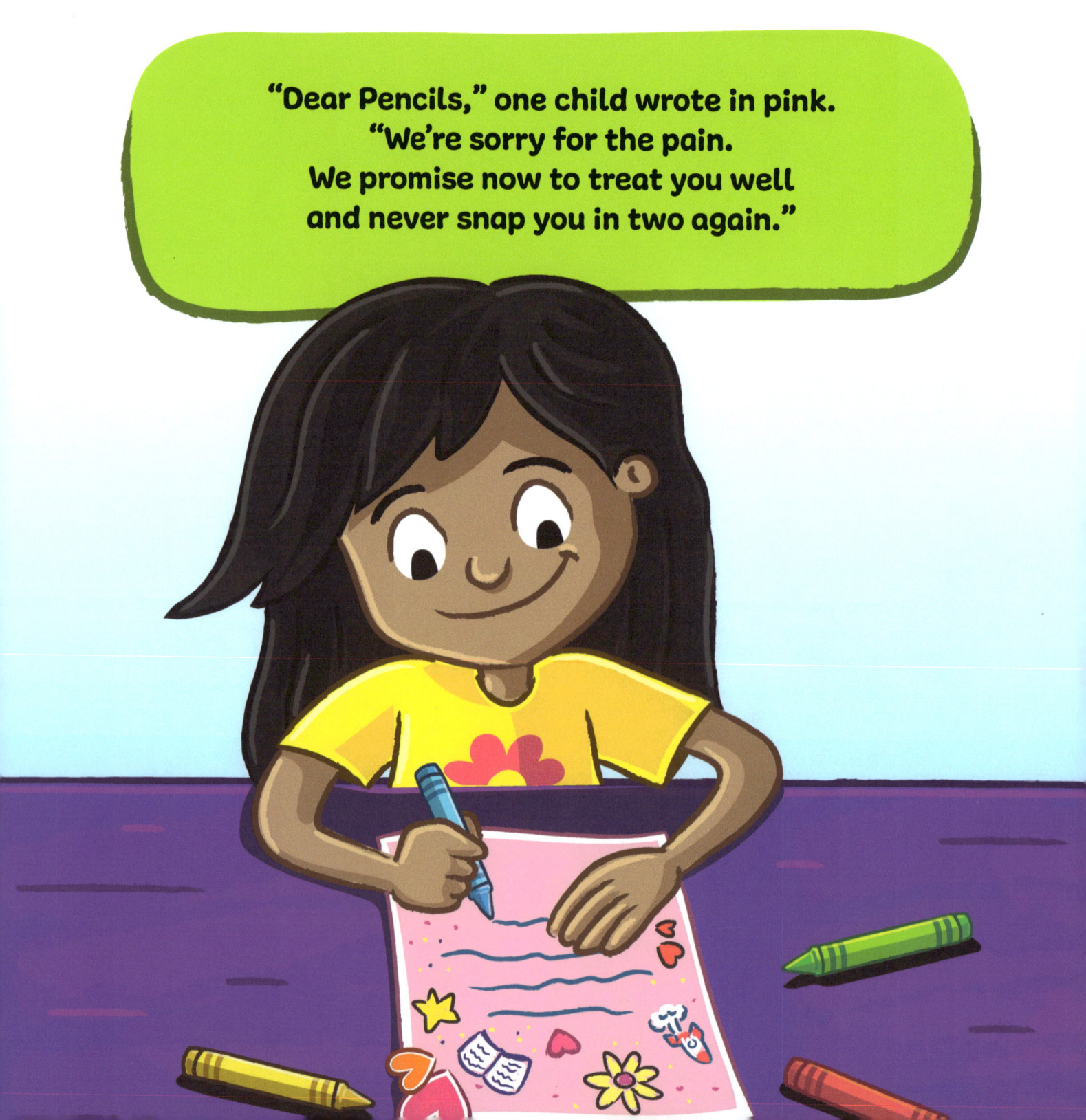

Another child sent a card
with drawings so neat and fine.
"We've missed you, Pencils! Please get well.
We'll see you hopefully in time."

The pencils at the hospital
began to feel much better.
The flowers brightened up their room.
They loved each single letter.

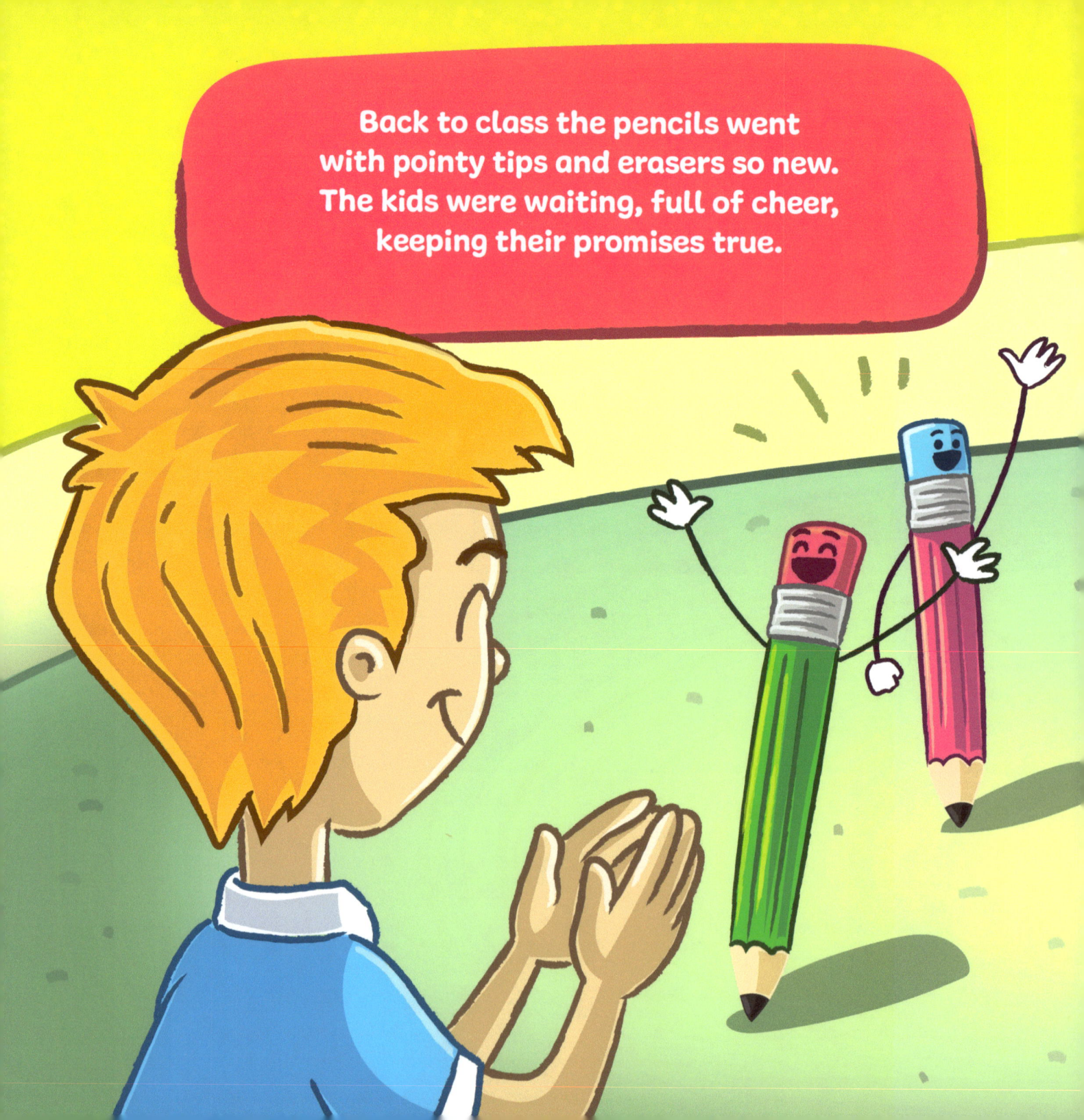

So if you have a pencil friend,
be kind and show you care.
Or else they might just fall ill,
to Pencil Hospital, oh beware!

No more chewing, no more snaps,
the pencils stood up tall.
They worked together, hand in hand,
and had the best time of all.

Now, every day the pencils write.
Their lines are smooth and clear.
The kids all learned to treat them right
and hold their pencils dear.

www.ingramcontent.com/pod-product-compliance
Lightning Source LLC
Chambersburg PA
CBHW041711160426
43209CB00018B/1801